Accounts of withdrawal

Poems in English taken

from

« Colourful Citations »

N·A·N·K·E

Poems

Poetica

Daydreaming

I jumped to satisfy my hunger, then higher
Through a storm of raindrops laced with thunder.
Now it's raining me, torn into pieces
Bits of flesh and bubbles of blood on a tree.
Now it's draining me.
Starts the rush to grow, born again in its flowers

It's not easy to soar when you're down
And it's much harder with your feet stuck underground.
Our body grows wider but the heart stays thin.
It still reaches higher hidden from sin.
If you need shelter, now, I'll slow down.
With my leaves I'll see to it that you're safe and sound

I can't forget looking at you even when you're gone
Keeping your image alive from afar.
Time runs so fast the sky blinks to the sun
Freezing the nights right down to their core
But we stood up to all, together
Still misery made us so bitter

We could meet again like two strangers
Who would have again to know each other
We still both, now, could face the dangers
But trust and love are easier with another

But we stood up to all, together
Still misery made us so bitter

And yet I can't forget looking at you even when you're gone

Peace at times

From a pile of dust rises an ashy phoenix
That crumbles in mid-air as said in the lyrics
Of a song sang for sleepy children of the west
Drunken by the speedy day and drowsy by night at best

It was a tale of conquest, a long and weary journey
Of a raindrop in a land of fire, of a god in a bird
That would come if you inquire help on wounded knee.
It would give life to all, to thousands, this was the third

Time passed and atrocities of yesterday ceased.
With them were hushed the jesters that'd dare say they seized
The meaning of the myth, so that history would sit
On a fluffy white pillow and so time took a hit

To erase war, illness and hatred we cast away all
And helpers, muses of glory and beauty last no more
Like water that would replenish a sea but bathe no shore
To ensure a future with no past
A present that would fail us...to fall

Standstill for a destitute prostitute

Slim slums mourn the sun by the rocky side
Slit by the cream that touched the riverbed
Through a bridge that hovers over the slim un-dead
Surrounding the heart that pumps fumes city-wide

As Terror led and wrote the infamous plague
A Play of many scenes for loyal lackeys lucky to die.
She lacked the lethal lead she tossed in the die
And fate had her run so citizens went rogue

A bounty on the fierce jackal that ruled the night
Was posted and thousands, in a hurry, were lured in
But the unruly rule and her land avoided the fight
Because green eyes met on the red carpet to the queen

With the voice of an angel

As we....
Blind hearts, bind hearts, build bridges, breed bitches
Cause demise, close doors, choose power, chase dollars
Deliver blows, discover weapons, decide futures, divide nations
Lie easily, lie above, love haters, leave winners
Mark masses, merk masses, mend people, mound bodies
Moan something, mean nothing, mess plans, miss targets
Pack heat, pick fights, play games, pay lovers
Run cities, ruin lives, rally killers, ready tombs
Slip often, stop rarely, stain icons, sustain wars
Tip scales, trap suckers, taste glory, twist words
Wreak havoc, wake disasters, waiver constantly, wander streets
And never care about the consequences
Or the causes and their threats
...A soft voice in the background said "smile for the camera"

Jack loving

I came right from the funeral, right after the ritual.
I am the perpetual critical chronicle of mutual burial.
I am the dialectical difference between artefactual and artifactual.
I am sceptical about the comical and satirical visual
Used to portray this animal as if it was stoical
When it's just your typical mortal cursing the mystical.
I'm just your tropical criminal out for the frugal
Joys of the practical tools brought to the superficial
Pleasures of small trinkets, almost like nothing at all.
Still I recall the tritical call echoed through fall

I remember your image, your composure and exposure.
I will wait to see you when it's time for the rapture.
I already know it's coming I don't need a lecture.
I capture the essence and the instance
Of the departure as I go the distance.
As I am quite sure you still must nurture your nature.
You rupture and your heart needs to mature in structure.
While comes the future
let me enjoy the pleasures of today's feature

Because when worlds collide, like when worlds divide
I still deny what the guide implied, I still stand aside.
As I subside with pride can I provide and prove
A law to which abide and still say I improve
When all I do is look above as I move
Picking with gloves the love in my heart I remove?
Therefore, before the semaphore loses meaning
Do say you'll reply to my incline as I am leaning.
I stoop to step on a steep slip, smitten by the slope
But I lose grip on your lip, please don't rid me of hope

Bella

I thought it was her name because she was beautiful
But when it came to her, peacekeepers had a mouthful
Because she was born in ancient Rome
And named after a war zone.
She was a weapon many hoped to hone
And a sin for which they'd atone

She was nimble in the rumble
And I would just tremble thinking of the implicit gamble.
You see, I am simply humble.
I would cower, fumble and crumble.
She was still a story, still a legend
When I came to stumble upon her fable

She had no equal, no one that was suitable.
She never liked the status in the quotes about her
Because of the status quo

She thought I was a soldier without a calling
Because I wasn't gunning for anything
In the epicentre of a power struggle between demons.
She simply watched, curious
About who would do something so dangerous.
I was nameless and it made her furious

I know there was nothing else to her but war
But I hoped for more
Though it was as hopeless as wanting
To see clear deep into a dark sea from the shore

She asked if I'd see her to the end
But I never fathomed there was more.
She left laughing thinking I'd feel shame and follow her for fame
But the thing, with games with guns and me

Is that I fail to take aim

Yet she still draws my eyes on her

I'm thankful for she put me back together
With parts that come out of her.
I thought there was no way out
But she pushed me out to let her be
And now we have to part though we're still the lovers we were

There was no near match that could light her fire.
One would hope, one day, men would tire of lusting for her
But there is no war from which men will ever retire

Oh, but she was beautiful, all dressed in ire

Bella, sorry for saying I don't need you, for being a liar

Streaming

In the morning, at my best for a strife
Programming the rest of my life
That still returns as a set of unresolved questions
All I'll try seems to be in the realm of unchecked actions.
So I just temporarily exchange two flags set to true
But I start running in parallel and cut through.
My memory leaks, one speaker blasts and speaks.
I'm overflowing, stuck with a stack at which no one peeks.
I know the key to this live lock, luckily I can still block.
Scanning through tracks and indices, I pointed out a free block.
All I wanted was residency in your main memory
But in the raid, I got swapped out to the redundant driver B.
I'm just slashes, hashes over addresses on the terminal.
That's why I have hooks on your every peripheral.
I'm in every entry, their head and their offset.
I sometime start where you stop and you're upset.
I won't let you get harmed whether it's your data or your tower.
I even delayed the wait to linger longer through your buffer.
Look, I know I haven't been in the loop.
Just give me one look, I'm just a noob skipping lines in a leap.
Sorry you must load so much as I stoop
To take bits off your time, just piling rhymes in a heap

Breathing

One more battle and I can finally exhale.
Hopefully, soon, I will prevail.
I can't wait for the next time I inhale.
Hail the frail that never fail
Neither himself nor in the battle in his trail
Even if he struggles to no avail
Even when none will sing his stale tale
Even when his last roar resounds as a wail

I'm holding my breath
In a state near death
To focus on meditation
To avoid hesitation.
I stop my respiration
Putting love in my reason
Killing the fire around me in its ignition
Never forgetting or forsaking the mission.
My foes are oblivious to my war, even allies turn to treason

Allow me to bring light to the rendition
Of the war in place, with your permission
For there is a time and a place for action
But never is it wrong for an explanation

My faction and I never will believe the fiction
Used in the terms of laws to enslave and condition
People opposed to segregation, to submission.
Who would accept such an abhorring aberration?

Of our own volition we will linger in this long transition.
We need preparation and ammunitions for this wild friction.
Rebellion is but a word when a people unites in opposition
In the late time for creation of foundations of a nation

I never had fascination for the apparition of an imitation.
I believe the revelation is the transformation
And any other association is an anticipation of annihilation.
May my determination never waiver in the weaving motion

Misinterpretation comes from the manifestation
Of the personification of a god
That is no more human and never was, for your information.
Infatuation of the fruition of our own imagination
Cannot be the solution to our desperation.
That discrimination is the very foundation of my elation.
I don't even care for the destination
I just go with the transportation

I hope this can be the inspiration of a new generation
To remember that concentration starts with relaxation.
Put a little dedication and motivation
In improving your perception.
It's easy, as long as you start your education with respiration

This is the integration of innovation in your obligation.
Thanks for your appreciation and your attention

....now breathe

After her

Hark you gods, don't you bark like dogs.
At least with luck you stand against the odds
I have a knack for making mistakes.
I can only turn on myself stakes and snakes

You hypocrites, what are you complaining about?
When you get any, then you can ask for more.
I lost the only thing I can say I would ever adore.
I believe everything about her, even my doubts

As first impressions go, she made the best I'll ever know.
I was hit straight to the heart and all in one blow.
She was like a gentle stroke on the day that was painted
As though kindness could be projected
On the blank canvas that forms now and after
And I wished that day would last forever.
I wished the sun wouldn't set on us
Then again, I can't lie, at night we would make a mess

May the sun be her throne or I will harness its power.
Watch, my beloved, as flies true this coward
Through the nothingness and the emptiness of space.
Watch as I haste only to once again be in her grace.
Let me bask in her light amidst the stars in the sky.
If I choose now, to side with Mars, don't ask me why

...If this is the last moment we spend together
I know it hurts, but save it; because I won't remember

It was ever since the very first night
That I took an oaf and became her knight.
She would look over my dreams
While I'm falling asleep in her arms.
Gently going across her skin with a finger, watching my breathing

Against the flesh of the evening.
I had fallen for all of her charms

The key to the release is on the chain that holds hostage my life
The brakes to quit are in the car that says "fuck your life"

...No I know better than to lose myself, the real me.
She was yet to be my muse and she amused me already.
I missed her coming. I miss her, now that she's gone.
I have to sever myself from the many drawn by the brawn

We clashed to have the last power.
We fought and lost the last wonder.
I list it all and ponder as we enter the last winter
The least of trophies given to the winner.

We were long in the wrong, I guess it's true we are strong.
How strange that I could hit the mark while aiming out of range.
I recall all the faces that we buried
But there is nothing I would change.
I can only sing along to the hymn of the land where we belong

They say life is good but for some being good is not living
But it isn't bad until you make out of death a living.
I knew what was right, but now what's left?
Nothing but these fists that can't fight, that have no heft.
I went on so hard to end up so soft.
You can now lift me with a waft

The sun still rises high in the sky and makes the air dry.
The land is crispy from the blaze.
We make a toast and it boils into a haze.
I fall in the vapour and get high

I am a picky florist, in my garden I remain very cautious.
I only have one flower; you wouldn't believe her...

How she's gorgeous
I'd rather wither if I can't be with her…
I went far after her...
Though it was vain, she's still what I prefer, out of what we were

At world's end

I'm laying in an empty room under a dimming light.
I'm saying words that resound in waves
That crash onto this world's end.
I'm fleeing to board the black ship of slumber
With in my ear, a friend.
I'm feeling merry while facing the hurdle of the day.
I'm losing grip of my hobbies, slowly falling in her favour.
I go on and on about the tiniest second and the next thing.
I fall back into the fleeting night
Of unspoken words that still cling
I feel I could never go down, lying down, still tasting your flavour

The roof, the root and the square root

The roof of paradise
Is the utmost passion, yet it's still but a phase.
It is nowhere near your thighs.
It has nothing to do with size.
For some it lasts only for a few days
And for those it ends with a surprise

The root of paradise
Is not a competition, it's a prize.
It comes when you fall in a haze.
You may struggle for it, but it comes with demise.
It is manifested in a pure blaze.
It's found by the good we demonize

But here it's the square root of paradise.
So we multiply until we realise
We are still the same number in disguise.
Still some come to pass, in this guise

We end up running to catch up the time that flies
But by trying to get a bit of paradise
We destroy bits off the high rise.
We lose our place and cut all ties.
We may wake up to realize we were not wise
But the excuses we make up are all lies

I have a long way to go, but in the meanwhile
I skip over the pain and go straight to laughter.
I never will regret the moments of now and after
Even when these last tend to go fast past
Even if they linger longer on my mind than they did last

The fetter

I see infinity as the next step
The unthought idea, the unfought battle
The unborn soul, the unbound layer
Where nothing is impossible, where nothing can stop
Where severed chains continue to rattle
Where my every scream is ended by a prayer

As I flutter along the way where my body should not wander
I'm bound by the fetter and any way I go all I do is wonder

It's a constant that fluctuates with vision
As one struggles to grasp it, it will still escape.
How fitting that the fetter would free me
Knowing that there is always better and that I could be free.
That I could be able to take any road and any shape.
That all I had to do is break my own prison

You are my fetter...

I should function without you but you are my nature.
Though you call me out it's always uncalled for.
You give me a fight and a battleground to sully
The power to support battle but still starve victory

The nourishing of the mind can never satiate
The hunger of the heart
And no thrust of the body can sooth the thirst of the soul
So I went looking for more ground to cover from pole to pole
But I still lost sight of you, I still ended getting deeply hurt

You are my freedom...

What am I to do if I cannot be free?
Where have you gone without me?

I break and I falter and fall in a gutter
Where I gut myself to find no other

I seek out no further pleasure
Than to be in your vicinity
And to do so, I go for it with no half measures
Because your are my infinity

The size of a king

The man woke up in a king sized bed.
He never wondered to know the fit to a king
And how such measure would be known by his underling.
He started to walk amongst his people that needed to be fed

He was much too kind
And gave all he could to his kind.
He wasn't afraid of the world
Not even when the unthinkable fate unfurled.

He didn't have a buck
But couldn't run out of luck
Had no pot to piss in
But had so much heart within

He wasn't versed in most matters
But he knew a verse from the last universe
The last words that made it too perverse
And could tell the tale of the town from its gutters

He held his crowd amazed with his quarrels
But he soon lost his crown and fell.
I wonder how that felt
As the last people knelt

The king was naked
The king was stupid
The king was a bum

He was already gone when most people forgot about him.
Some asked around, looking for him, when they found him
They realized he had fooled the lot of them.
They were puzzled, lost and furious
But then fury is quick to take the best of us.

The king lost touch. He never had much
He could have returned but never did as such

That man was a distance in any direction.
He was way too big but way too little for his own passion.
It is only when you're ready for the surprise
That you can open and never again close your eyes

The happening

My heart is hewn from the most unsightly mounts of rocks.
In tune with most songs of unforgiving foes in mere boondocks
Populated by a few good men
My city stands with much fortitude.
Many times its regular beating would give birth to my anxietude.
Can I fathom living such a phantom life
When I see the unfurling of my fate?
Will I make it in time to get where I belong, or will I be too late?

I was deserted, disheartned, alone in the desert
Alone in the flow of words
Coming from my dissing and hissing hollow heart.
But in that desert with noises was an oasis made of quick sands
From a paper in my think tank where the ink sank
Where nonsense stands

I just thought of meeting the right person
With the right complexion and the right diction
On the same path and direction to some addiction.
I thought I'd be better off but I began to worsen

It was happening...

The quickening of seeds into towers
That blossom with flowers that roam walls and halls

I never thought we would fight
That whatever each of us said would be right.
Shots were fired but this was cold war gun play
Sharp wordplay that was akin to swordplay.
I thought we were serious but all we did was foreplay

I've been trying. I've been tried
But still trials fill my path
Obscuring it with wrath.
I never knew how salty tears could be when I cried

The sun was brighter ever since that day begun
Drying and dying my mouth with colours on the run
And then came another asking to live our lives together
But I was still trying to put my life together

I wanted her to be like fire, to be boundless
And take my breath away with her dance
To intoxicate me with her soul broken into flinders
For she's the incentive to my body of cinders

What charmed me is not her body in motion
Neither the light emitted nor the heat radiated
It was what moved the form that had me bewildered.
It was the course of consumption.
It was the art and the dance of shedding life
The making of a peace, the simmering of strife

Who are we?

The point I am at, the point I am getting at
Is that, even my mother won't know where I come from.
It's to the point where my feet won't know where I'm going.
It is not based on a simple and pitiful spat.
I am not who they think I am at home
And they may think that I have done nothing
But bring my undoing

There is a time and a place for things we soon replace
But where can I find the dreams and beliefs we put away in wait.
I say they drive the very passion that we sought elsewhere
It is then not a sense of direction but a need for pace
That will set a different mood and fool you into going straight
While, ahead, you may realize you actually went nowhere

You say I lose my time, but I do it all watching it pass.
You say I waist my skills, but you have no idea how I hone them.
You say I need to be more focused on a culture and a people
But all you really want is for me to let things go while I'm idle.
I do not need to idolize anyone's merits or anyone's class.
You do not recognize me
Because you mistake the tree from which I stem

Can you hear the tear in my laughters?
Can you see the smile in my tears?
Can you feel the distance in my embrace?
Can you appreciate the coarseness in my grace?

Well, can you? Are you deaf, blind or simply insensitive?
Do you miss the point or its incentive?
Should I dumb myself down? Or can you keep up?
Actually, I wouldn't be able to take it if you could.

Believe me, I don't think you should.
It would only be a constant bother.
I wouldn't stand for you to be another
And yet to know all of whom I am so far
When I can't do the same with who you are

In fact, that's my problem: I don't get you
And I wish not to feel so powerless
So I wish you the same inaptitude and shortcomings.
It is my way to tell you with much cowardice
That we don't need to know everything.
So, you're asking "who are you?", but I'm asking too

They're among us

The ones you wish you knew
The ones you failed to meet
The ones you cannot defeat
The ones with whom you grew

The ones you once loved

The ones you thought you freed
The ones you agreed to lead
The ones rooting, still, for you
The ones waiting, still, for you

Those ones are but a few
But they are here for you
And we're all looking at the horizon.
We wonder: will you redden the sky?
We don't even wonder why
This could be our last season

Do you even have a reason for this madness?
Where has gone all the kindness?
How did you become so furious?
How could you fool those wiser among us?
How could you threaten those weaker among yours?
I hear that tonight it might rain
And when it rains it pours.
Careful to whom you send pain

We had all the time in the world for one last prayer
One last thought
So are you going to drop the bombs or not?

Pure

Have the heavens fallen for a schmuck?
Why should I be stricken by such luck?
That there'd be a love so empty
That it'd weigh on my soul plenty
That there'd be nothing to gain from it
Neither right nor power lay in its pit

And as well up in me the belief
That swells from each of my pores with no relief
That it is obviously the most pure of all
I realize it is the only cure that made me fall

Alas it serves only the nourished soul
At last, I see why hunger has me still whole

This new affliction must be a play on the poor.
If not, what is to do the son that it bore?
This rebirth is the unleashing of a new breed
Born to reap earth and replenish it with a new greed

Safe to say, I never agreed to this fleeting phantom.
It surprises me that in this state I would fathom
This notion, for I fall for any so seldom
When I know love touches at random

Void of the meaningless spices we throw at it
Love is the groundless reason to sweep us off our feet.
It is the unforeseen season that follows once we meet
It is the only reason why I care, if even one bit

Clumsy lover

I need ink in my mouth to say the words of my fading youth
In a mother tongue I don't speak fluently without looking aloof.
Any wider and the pen, still mightier than the sword
Will take out a tooth.
Any wilder and the sharks in these steel waters
Will swim through my roof

I'm standing in the light of an unusable payphone
Posted outside the booth.
I've been meaning to talk to you and though I haven't
That's the truth.
Forget the missing and the missed times
I could have multiplied with happiness
Quality time was just so hard for me to qualify for.
This much, I can confess

It's still spring as I rehearse how to utter the silence in this pause.
It's still too early for a summer fling, too late to hide my flaws
But I heard a call from behind me, it sounded like your voice
So I responded with a ding throughout the universe
Even now, I rejoice

Still, I look outside and peek inside to find myself a bit uncouth.
I have yet to rest, much wells up to hit and cover my dry shores.
I keep counting the keys left so much I forget there are no doors.
I am but a rough gem rolling onward.
On my way out, I will be smooth

Restless uncivilised people

Picture weapons drawn on the damned poor
Kept developing in their downfall
Left stranded after a moot last call
With teeth clanking in the downpour

They had immaculate souls with a skin bloated with soot
Tangled up with unknown threads in the form of a suit
Given a rotten and yet still forbidden fruit

Dancing in circles around a fire
Flaunting sore knuckles and desire
Mumbling words narrated through legends
That become twisted and unspoken.
Meaning that is lost through translations
Between generations and populations
Of warriors of metal with spears at the ready
With cloths we smear with a rain tainted and bloody

While commemorated shields rest in peace
History will without a doubt stay in one piece
But it will fade in the memory of men
As crumble the mementos erected with this pen

Born to mourn those bred and dead
Sworn to an oath to a scorned oaf
Blind and bound to fall dead ahead.
You can see the lost losing because of thinking it's a given
That something has to got to give to be forgiven.
You can see a fool committing the most fouls of acts in folly
To have his story written with the rest of history

The throne is but a chair but many kill to be the heir.
This life is harsh to the weak
Where daily bread is a winning streak

Well, nobody will

I ask of her to love me properly
She says she doesn't know how.
I ask of her to explain her endearment.
She says she doesn't get why

I ask of her to share her dreams.
She says she never thinks of them.
I ask of her to let down her guards.
She says she doesn't control herself

I ask her if she can trust me.
She says she trusts nobody.
I ask her if she doesn't want more.
She says she didn't know she had any

Well I say there isn't much to hear.
She says it's nothing really, nothing to fear.
Well I say it's nothing I can bare.
She says I am not fair

She says she doesn't see how to live.
I say she doesn't know why we love
And if nobody has the will
Well, nobody will

I'll remember about you

The fidgeting when you're wet
The way you hide that you sweat
The way you cleanse yourself with dirt on your mind
The way you come undone when you remember I don't mind
The way you used to let me pour my every thought into your ears

I'll remember how you made me feel crazy
Crazy love, crazy strength, crazy days.
I will remember how you made me happy
Even now, I fall at times in that crazy daze

Though, you thought I wasn't looking and only listening
I kept it all etched in the deepest parts of my soul.
I hope when I scratch the surface I won't make a hole.
I want to remember you still, for me, you were unending

At the show

I was but a mere spectator in a dark room that was filled
With laughter and clapping that become applause
Where one side was lit to put under a spotlight if not a tight spot
Voices that indeed needed to be heard

My friends and I really loved your performance.
I have only love and respect for you.
Please stay as colorful and sweet
And may fate and the world be kind to you
As it is clear that you have but kindness in you

I was snapping and clapping at the truest words ever spoken
While we whispered our discomfort
For we are of the world that has rotten

I cannot dismiss the moment for the people that smile in it.
I got excited but not quite inspired.
They were things I want to hear, see and feel
Because they were things already inside of me.
They now have a medium through which I channel.
This was me on stage. That was my standing ovation

The other side

It's winter in the room by the river.
Like waiting for another tide
I listen to you laying on the other side.
It all started because I lied.
I still have plenty that I hide

Every sound you make falls in my ears.
Every move you make pressures my core.
My eyes blind through the day
Pierce the blurry shades of grey
Of the moonlit drapes dancing
On your sheets that keep moving

You snore, grind your teeth
Roll, toss, turn... I need relief.
I bite my heart that pounds up and through my throat.
I pace my breathing but I'm still distraught.
In vain I wait for you to approve
In my moot silence, I don't dare move

I'll convince myself that I'll stay lonely.
It'll work because that's my daily story.
And the morning comes like you weren't there
And the day will end and I will not fare.
It's already too much for me to bear.
I already can't get myself to care.
I can't dare lose you in the dead of night.
I know, now, that is never to be my fight

Your birth

The clattering of dishes
Glass in broken pieces
Salty water under marshalled breaths
Words that seep through unsightly spaces between teeth
While a cry and tears mix into a bubbling foam of rage
The call for help, the urgency, the bright eyes
Wet skin, skinship, coos
The light that brightly makes the emptiness shiny and anew
The moment the one became two

That miracle was you
That was your birth
And your mother was alone, waiting
Wanting, hurting, dying, giving birth

The succubus

Adding a touch of haze on the hazelnut
Her incandescent gaze fell on the have and have not.
Her indecent descent brought more dissent
Among an already dissident people.
Then again, even she was blind to the stir
Really, an imperious marvel.
The fells were filled with fools that fell for her

I found myself in her room
As though my head did not lead
As though I had paid no heed.
A pity, that pretty soon, a little room
All the freedom in which to roam
Kills the little men in it

The fiercest was the fairest.
A siren, I would have her and sire a son.
I was mad with desires.
I was consumed by vile fires.
With no haste, no wait and no waste
I went for her waist

Her touch was a paradise
A mire of lost breaths
Lost souls and lust.
The salience of my insolence
Suddenly broke her silence.
My salvation was the lack of resistance

More amble in the amber embers of her fire
The shadows ran on the walls of her defences
And the course of her veins.
The blood aloud in the south
Aloud in her mouth

She screamed, while beating the drum in her heart
While I tired beating the drum on her flesh

With leaden pulses, heavy strokes
The moon carried me back and forth
Under her gentle light.
That night I had sight but no insight

With the tide's ebbs and flows
My rock was but sand on her shores
And I swam in her waters where tears are meaningless.
And the moon still shined.
And the moon still waned

Already on the brink of breaking the hinges
She flinched, she clenched her thighs
Quenched her thirst and in one burst...

She didn't put up a fight.
She just silently closed her eyes.
She moved one of her fingers in the palm of my hand
But that was all of her might.
That was all she could do tonight

All she did was move
Move on top of me, move beside me.
She lit a fire, a blaze that would consume me at night
And the ashes, I still taste them in my mouth.
That's all I can taste.
The feeling that I could do anything
Wraps me whole like a blanket.
It robs me of my mind and fills my thoughts
And I wake up in the stupor
Of a lonely reality
Of a lonesome future

It's all the same

The skies are in the water and there is water in the skies.
I wish I could say there was none in my eyes.
It pulls at my heart to see you fight at each chance.
It breaks my heart to see you do it crying at each glance.
I listen for your voice but hear nothing
Then you call out my name and I forget everything.
I put on hold holding onto those I hold dear
As my fear of time unfolding lasts another year.
My path darkens with blight but with insight I steer clear
Of the echoing howls in the hollow sky that draws near.
My every move is welcomed but is insincere
But your every inquiry comes in only to sear
What little piece of flesh that I have, to keep me whole
The last piece that's attached to my soul.
Whether I went to you or whether you came
When we end up apart it's all the same

She had been suffering

She had been lying
In that white room with musky air
And nobody would say it
But lingering was the smell of death

Her frail hands
With a needle in the finger
Her frail arms
With a needle in the crook of her elbow
They took me in a slow embrace

There was no past
We were already looking ahead
Little time and little room
But we were looking at that instead

Brushing off and shrugging at old inquiries
And with a simple smile forgetting old injuries.
I look by the window
There was nothing beyond it
It could have been any season
Any day, any year
As though time meant nothing
Even if that room and that time
Was all we could have
All we could share

There was no past
We were just looking ahead
Little time and little room
But we were looking at that instead

We shared short stories of long gone days
Quick quips about a gone wrong phase.

Sometimes, as though we wanted to laze around
We'd sit in silence, as long as we both stuck around

She had been suffering.
She had been strong.
She always had been.
Nobody was in the wrong

We were not looking at the past.
We were just looking ahead.
Little time and little room
But we were looking at that instead

Safe Sax

Blues and Jazz
Nothing safe about it

The rhythm had the walls shaking.
The floor was on the brink of breaking.
The heat would strike at our flesh
Undoing the knots our minds would mesh

Close and personal the music wouldn't leave
Played through a scorching summer
With a dimming light and soft chatter
With a few surprises from under a sleeve

It would come at the ear
Let in with little to fear

The feeling made us nostalgic

We would bump into the night
Taken onto a quick flight
Through evening air and bright lights.
Novelty still failed to feel trite

Unpredictable, unrelenting
Like sparks from a fuse
He would play for the muse.
The fingers would be lit.
The sax would be a hit

With little vice and little innocence
The body would talk
And souls would listen
Not too many were present
But there was a strong presence

The last movement took me far
To a hill atop the city
And the moon shan't hide
Shining amidst clouds in its stride

Without being rude he'd still be impudent
Tonight was tender and decadent

Stark naked in his notes, it was evident
He was no pretender, he was confident

A light graze here
A wink there
The instrumental was clear, the sorrow unfair
A token from a man that was broken

Yet unbowed, his frame said the unspoken
Trying to pull himself together
Trying to put his life together

I was taught you get tit for tat
So I tipped my hat and tipped in the hat

Blues and Jazz
Nothing safe about it

Gardening

White nights that resume
When ends the next day
Dark flowers that bloom
In darks rooms with gloom?
I'll have a bouquet

The thorns I consume
Cut me from inside but I assume
That feeling is lost in the fumes
Of the fire and shadow of death that looms

I presume this perfume
Is not the life that lingers
It's the one out of reach
Ever escaping my fingers

Another wall I must breach
Another body I must teach
Nothing I should preach
But I've had enough practice

Things break fast before breakfast
When we move fast into bed head first

This won't end soon
This won't end well

As I did for the beautiful flowers I cut from the garden
I swore I wouldn't have you wither.
I realize how prised you were to me

Sweet lies under blue skies make for odd ties

At last my first

It was just the last time but that was my first.
I should move on and give it a rest
But I did my best at my worst

I had my first at last.
I thought the thirst would pass.
Good things don't last.
Good thing that was ass.
Good thing that was us.
You bet I would bust.
It wasn't about the trust
You knew that was lust.
A little less about guts
A little more about actions and cuts.
The passion makes us nuts

Get gone if you must.
The only pressure I feel is in the thrusts
Though the bed might break as it adjusts
To things we do that call disgust

Those looks seem unjust
In the middle of the desert we are but dust
Our ashes rise as we consume and combust
Taken by a gust of wind

We went too fast the last time.
We may last longer this time.
This was surely my first
But you may still be my last

If this is about you
What does it say about me?

Powerless

It's too late to tell fate how to unfold
As tomorrow comes before the story is told.
Whether we can or can't weather warm days
That bump into the night and turn cold
Armed with the galls to throw out the old
And the wit to do it without getting too bold
We were given models and a map to string our steps
But we were of another mold.
We were told to shine but we were rather more inclined
To be concrete than to turn to gold.
The latter is more malleable
And we were made to stand our ground
But something even that strong cannot hold.
It would weigh on us
And though appalled we were asked
To fall back again into the fold

The following

A man not from above
Of little words
Came to say what came before
And he had a following

...

And I was there to listen
But I heard the following

...

And that was the end

I once followed and was thorough
But I envied the bird in the sky
So I put one in the barrel
Found two in a bush
Lost pace and peace in the rush
Used red to paint the quarrel
And it came out through the brush.
I never was lax so the last coat was lush.
I turned an idol into a rival.
I turned to a rebel and made him revel.
I worked through the pain and played it subtle.
I kept building to never quite settle

I was not fast enough
To pursue happiness or run from my sorrow
And I would run into you but not my tomorrow

I told the following
Not to fall in
But stand out
To go all in
And reach out
And if we fall through
To pray we don't fall out

To stay grounded
But take flight

That's how sounded
Our first fight

What comes before
Was said to the following
And when there were more
They just kept coming

We Won't End

Life comes so soon
Once in a blue moon
Everything is just right.
I wish the moon was blue tonight
But here we are now.
That was quite the performance
That was quite the last dance
You can take a bow

Levity in my words may not convey the severity of the situation.
Brevity is alas not the remedy
And though I must keep it concise I still need to excise
The meaning behind the mess
The woman under the dress and the man in duress

Surprisingly and strange enough I care for this terrible folly.
I can't help but imagine that this crazy notion with the right push
Enough people and a bit of luck
Could very well give birth
To an unprecedented wild wish and dream

Could I be half of everything
And keep diving myself to reach infinity?

I stared into your eyes that said all these things I couldn't perceive.
I wound up coiling back from their depths.
That day, if only for that day
I wouldn't have minded being blind
But the sight is etched in my memory
And sinks pulling all I know in a spiral
That will soon spin me
And hurl my boundaries into an implosion
No one will witness.
I owe it all to my weakness.

I try to go to sleep and come to mind
All the places where I want to be
All the people I want to meet, all the things I want to do...
And the saddest part is that I am not dreaming yet...
Even sadder than knowing I won't remember my next dream.
Just leave out all the rest.
Put it all to rest.
Just remember our love.
Just remember I'll love you

Eternity can fit in a single instant
While it becomes ever so distant.
It doesn't have to be at the edges or in between
It just has to be when you give in

What the mind forgets
The body might remember.
Within the reach of each other
With about enough patience, tenderness and warmth
We might make it.
This could be the defining moment
We needn't know it. We'd tell, always
And it would last forever
In that single point in time and space
Somewhere, some day.
We were tightly woven around one another
In an unbreakable thread of our intertwined fates
The string of our joined lives
The chance meeting of lost souls
That were bound to cross.
Even history had to repeat itself
Or make minute corrections.
For centuries, stuck in a loop.
Everything might end
But thanks to just this, we won't.
Let us believe it even if all others don't

Wild ride

I have a way with otherwise wise words
Whatever those may be

Maybe they already have me away
Otherwise I am with you

Where have you taken me?
I lost track of time
When I found myself taken by you

I started a cold war of shots made in wordplay
As sharp as cuts from swordplay

I won the armor I wear in the battles
That left me brittle underneath
And I carry now the worst scars beneath

A waft after the breeze wakes me
In screams amidst debris

A wall rises as you set for another sun
And you swoon under a new moon
And the lackluster light.
But I take flight because I cannot take the fight

What was I even trying to do?

I mesh a web of lies for the few times
I feel the need to turn back.
I know there are times you will want me back

I wet my cheeks with weeks of sorrow.
If I seem weak and meek today, I won't tomorrow.
I will weave back the strands and this time I will be thorough.

I will make a cloth that fits the man I am
So if I look divested you will have caught me changing.
I will to keep my wits as I catch a whiff of your perfume
And I attempt unknowingly to weed out
From which direction I may spot you
In the loud crowd of the people that were left out

I am letting go of the wheel
Drive me to where I can still revel and feel
I have the time to kill and the zeal to reveal
How to reel in something real

Luckely I still wake up to find myself at your side
I guess I get one more round on a wild ride

In the pit

The world I aspire to depict is but a tick of the clock
A knot in the thread of which the likeness plays out
Only once every turn
Regardless of how many there could ever be

The vacuous fill that has the surface glistening
Over the similar still has me wondering
If I may stretch my intoxication
To flatter the rather flat membrane
Where permeates the illusion of separation

I try to keep my heart still
But it beats to no end.
I attempt to clear my mind
But a single thought fills it

Often you moved me to tears.
At times you'd remind me of my fears.
Many times I saw you still.
The last time almost didn't feel real
I catch myself with your image on mind, still

This is not because of what I saw.
I was blind to the most beautiful vision
Deaf to the greatest call
This is my fall.
While nears the wither of winter
My fire is but a cinder.
The party is well but over.
My youth has ran its course.
I am now but older.
I let my feathers fly and fetter sink.
I do not love anymore
I rather think

The children of music

After a while, the winds would learn of every corner
In the city and a howl would resonate
And sound stronger on the walls
Of buildings as though playing
A colossal and terrifying instrument.
The music played was none other than that of demise.
The power was soon out, the heat too and fear was free
Roaming the confines of minds and running wild.
The peril was that the people would give in
And give up the little hope they were given
For any rope they could find to hang themselves with
Rather than hang in there.
Unable to see a thing outside
Their gaze would turn inwards
Onto an abyss that knew not to look back
And they would plunge, some to their death, no matter the depth
And the breath of the ripper would mix
With the smoke from dying fires
Lit in an unforgiving cold
On floors that were not meant to bear heat.
Was it day? Was it night? Clocks had stopped ticking
The last watch was for a fellow
That had fallen into slumber while crept malice at the doors.
But none dared blame him.
Dreams of warmth would take away those too cold.
But the watch needn't be bold.
The watch was quickly made of old as the young died fast.
First to respond to attacks and partake in vengeance.
The infants would be last and they would be found
In the middle of the dreadful music
At the bowels of the instrument

That city there

Foaming from the lips
Near The mound, at the mouth
I say that coming in.
I say that getting out.
I stay silent in between.
My neck breaks at each corner.
My voice curves and swerves
As I call and cuss for a caress.
My hand stretches but my need is not met.
With everyone I encounter
Even when I sit long by the counter.
The music and light
Loud and bright
Won't let me sleep through the night

I don't remember the sun coming out.
I only recall how I stayed out.
All night at all hours
Looking for yours, out of ours

I was lost in that city there.
I couldn't breathe its heavy air
So I only pass for so long.
I know I don't belong
And I curse my thirst.
I rage at my hunger
For the girls in that city there
Far from where I fare

The city was my fear of intimacy.
I was feeling that distance
Couldn't let love grow
So I would see things I never saw
And believe things I never knew

I know I am unfair
To that city there.
I don't trust the people in it
Neither the water nor the law

I have cold feet when I think about it
And few things could make them thaw

The games we play

Because the parallels do not seem to cross your mind
I have to try and lead you here as though you were blind

You weighed heavy on my mind
And when I stick my neck out
I lose my head.
What would you have me do instead?

I never lacked luck sitting on bone.
I never broke one throwing the first stone.
My misfortune was to pay attention without caution.
To make good tricks one relies on confusion and deception

We were but lovers under covers
With a lot to give so we gave it up

You've been dying for attention
But I've heard you come alive
Where you're gonna live

You love me
You long for me
You cut me short
You cut me deep
You loathe me
And I, you

I put you to pieces
And when I came to pick you up
The puzzle was incomplete.
Something was missing.
I guess things will never be the same

The games we play
End with foul play

Love is blind
But if I only look at you
What can I expect to see?

Must I tie a knot
To find you love me not?
Can I say my piece?
Can you be my peace?
Just say your word
And become my world

With a light caress I ingress and sink into skin.
I have no qualms about it
I was always generous in sin

Strange beasts that ran through the fray
The game kept some just so they would play.
So she would cast a stone and stay a stone throw away.
The games we played always ended with foul play

To a bonfire

I want to see the flames of your passion rise ever higher
And your shadow to stretch into a thread
That will touch the edge of infinity.
I want you to shine as bright as the first and last light.
I want your warmth and your scalding touch in the depths
Of the soul you already etched.

I want the world to dare put you out
And tire in front of your undying fire.
I want the last thing I see to be your blaze
Even if that makes me blind

Pending attachment

Deeply rooted by the storms
The beauty lied in the thorns
As wolves crept closer
Skipping between depressions in the snow

The signal of the sinew, told me of what would ensue.
A slow slew fell by a few fellows no quicker and no better.
In a paradigm that hinders them, what would the poor pursue?

The waves would take my words
On the sand and carry them in the sea.
I hope the meaning is not lost
In the translation as it is my intention
To reach her even if she was at world's end in another dimension

Soon I cross the plains
And across she pains.
Alas her loss makes her paint
An empress with emboss about to faint
And the feint glow off its gloss
Lingers on my mind as I turn and toss
Looking to meet her eyes
Waiting to hear her laugh
To drop my lies and shed my guise.
If she would be my half
Then in her behalf
I would keep at bay her fears
And tend to her whims and ills

She appeared out of nowhere
Without sound, out of thin air
And with a laughter
That had her blush
She broke the silence that mixed

With the buzzing of bees stuck
In the ventilation
Drums resounding out in the hall
And the rustling of leaves by the windows.
Soon it was fall

We almost lost it all
Almost lost each other.
I stayed to get her
Until we'd get together

I am wearing the smile she gave me
Still weary from the heavy pain that came with it.
I, too, will bury my mark deep inside her

The light is dim and the culprit is my wit
As I try to change the mood if even one bit.
I remember her scent of carnations
And our bond beyond carnal through reincarnations

Teeming with an undying spirit
That draws on the eye what cannot possibly be seen
As though she was planning to hide in plain sight
Her cloth was nature itself.
She was divested, that was the truth.
Her hair would twist in the wind and string me along.
Unlike smitten kittens let loose in silky linens
Because of giggles she makes a rut out of riddles.
The complex was her wish to make it simple
But no man knew to buy without a sample.
They were lost when the message was too subtle
And didn't last when they would mess around
Before they would struggle.
But behind the bend
You could find her bound
Frozen in fear at the lost and found.

Again, I get twisted between lines that unblur
As unfurl the words and builds a stir
In the turmoil of strides
Surrounding a sunken gem:

I have to break the habit of breaking up with her

We would make love

Odds stacked against me
And I'm peeking
But all I see
Is that I'm peaking

Running laps around relapse
Taking notes of spots to stop
I backtrack to get back on track
From picking fights for topics
And attempt to refrain from a repeat
And switch lanes before I am to blame
But I see the turn in view
The crash around the corner
Bound by a perverse bend in bed
That has me taking a turn for the worse

Something was up and it was only morning
She had been getting sick right about this time

I was taking her somewhere
Because I had to be there
And she was here
And I could speed without fear

I have spent half my life in a bottleneck
I admit to still be a wreck
And I may feel the water rise
And she tears up in surprise
As she loses her water
As she loses her daughter

I understand I am only a stand-in
But I will withstand all for her
And hand in hand, we will make a stand.

Months ago, she sat on the crown.
That year she would crown.
That day she would drown
In a flood of tears.
That day two would die.
Another day, another die

In between smiles she would frown
But in a few months she would try again
Shedding a few tears here and there.
I wonder will I manage to drown
In the middle of the screams and pain?
I wonder, is there something to gain?

I see how they look at us.
I can tell how they had us.
I know now love made us
And in turn we will make love

Rock, Paper, Scissors

With apt words in the face of the surly bonds of life
I have been steadily gaining strength in view of strife

I have been on my way.
I never lost my ways
But I still lost myself on the way
On occasion, for a few days

I keep on dancing to the instrumental.
I keep on lusting for this dime
That you think is a doll
But dull swords never had the glory or the gall
To find out which leaves stayed green through fall

She was the whetstone, the sharp edge of my all.
I blame her for my zeal and the weight of my steel.
For her, I'll stall my time to shine into a still

The potter molds clay
To meet the painter one day

She was the model.
She was the star.
She was my rock
Then I got paper
But she threw tantrums
When money lost momentum
So I cut her off
With the scissors

I have been trying to not remember
Things I already forgot
And times spent saying there was none.
Those times are fully wasted.

I thought I forgot to breathe
But she took my breath away.
There was nothing I could do about it

The sound of my flesh sinking
Into hers, still echoes in my ears.
It was stronger than my fears
And grew stronger with years

It's not fair that few fare this far without fear
Where if you can't stand, you're told to stand clear

She was my rock
But it's been rocky ever since

I was nowhere, I am now here

Second breath

I am not shy of my affiliations
I heard the allegations about the altercations.
I have many musings about the troubles that I mention
Because they brought me up faster than the nation
And I was caught going through the motion.
When I talk about the evil that should have us tread with caution
Notorious and nefarious demons come to mind

Recall the deeds that went unpunished in the dissention.
Looking high waiting for ascension
Many get stuck on their knees untrue to their devotion.
It's abhorring but pay attention to the pretension.
At the point of no return, it will bring about utter destruction.
The beauty of the veil is but a distraction.
True colors shine when a clear canvas accepts creation

Mesmerised by apparitions apparently some pay for the adulation.
It's just an abomination that in addition
Comes to undermine the conviction
Of those with little faith but great alienation

It was due to the desperation facing an unfathomable application.
The streets were shaking with agitation
And the fence fell flat in front of the opposition
And often the solution seemed continuous absolution.
Souls were up for auction
Some sat while, at the doors, there was action

It was no simple aggravation
We were done in by aberration.
The words were lost in the citation
And there was no recognition
Of what could be the vision.
The blind were left in the dark

And the mute met with moot oblivion
While the deaf were told of consolation

The verb was unknown but bred the faction.
Our nature was bound to show function.
We let go of the very convention
That love could suffer corruption.
There was no room for any correction
The error was to be blind in the face of perfection.
And the cumulation of our wishes
Became the culmination of our efforts.
And the inclination in our voices
Gave birth to a new generation

I request dedication for the cause
It is with emotion that my erudition
Turns into an eruption with the escalation
Of the situation of what we built as a foundation
But no erection could reach so high without oppression

No exemption was made
My exertion was felt in the execution
And expectations went from explanations
To excuses, broken dreams and apologies

The expiration was written long before creation
The expiation lies within that notion

Another world was painted through the fascination
And this gave form to an idea that would blur our vision
But those who took a look could not deny
How distorted it was and how void of meaning
Was the corresponding action

I feel no frustration, my fixation had me reach my destination.
The foundation lasted enough for the gestation.

I cooed, cried, called and I finally answered without hesitation.
I have the gall and gumption
To show that we are all gifted.
My elation went passed any inhibition
And the imitation was short-lived because of superposition

My inaction was my full plan in action
And the inception was the same citation
That hid the incantation but was revealed through induction.
The mind only calls for instruction
This is my humble dedication.
Let it be the second inspiration.
A little mediation at the crossroads of innovation and obligation

Pardon the transgression
My intention was not an intervention
Nor an interjection in the discussion
You started before this revolution
But my intuition calls for an introduction
And each iteration is an invitation to jubilation.
The music sits on a cosmic partition.
The tune may remind some of perdition

This is my position and petition.
As I stand behind my prediction
I make the subtle proposition
Despite potential retaliation
That I know no reserve or restriction
More unbearable than ignoring salvation
And falling for seduction and temptation
For satiation is not of this world.
The transition is my vocation.
Take part of the transportation

I dare love, lost within damnation

Courtship for the dumbfounded (My heart goes to you)

As awkward as it may seem I couldn't refrain
From putting my foot in the door at the cost of shooting it

I have little flair
But maybe you can get a sense
Of my flow in these flowers

I was but a minstrel out for morsels for my musings
And I was given the luxury of an odd vagary.
I am just a stranger with the random inquiry
Of what you are about and your past whereabouts

Given the choice I will use my vernacular.
How else can I try to set high the bar?

I find that you have been pulling at my heart strings
And now like the instrument of my own demise it truly sings.
And I would like to try to be as bold
As to give you my heart to hold

I can no more clear my thoughts that you clutter
With each and every part of you that I discover

Entertain the proposition that I indeed am in love.
You decide if it's going to be pleasant.
Excuse my pessimism but romance
Only got me the last dance
And I never know when's my last chance.
So kindly come hither before I whither

And I debut with a debit
Professing my passion with profusion is my damnation
But I hope it turns out to be your addiction

As you bring me the greatest elation out of all of creation

I cannot quite make out what you are about
So I shorten the distance
Flatten the fence
Ready my defence
And give you a shout

Let me propose that you would be my ideal and let me deal
With what makes you think it cannot be real

The utmost compliment you could return to me
Is if you said I complement if not complete you

I would like you to consider the idea
That if you would grant me the pleasure
Of growing my soul in the fields of yours
I would come to encounter
The wonders that move you
And that would surely move me
And transport me to unseen heights of happiness
That I could never repay for
If not with unending affection

If you shall take my hand
I will never let go of yours.
And if I can't keep you near
I want to make clear
That you can take that hand and go for however far you desire
For I will stretch my reach
To the ends of the world, even through fire

The world is but a quantum of space when our souls meet
And each quantum of time remains etched
In my memory when our souls mate

If you deem me unworthy of these words.
Witness my trial and watch me err.
Humor me so that I may return the favor

I rise with a steady incline
Towards the sky, towards you.
If I shoot at the stars scattered out in the dark,
And land on your moon will it have you swoon?

I reckon I could lose myself to passion
If even for one short instant
To linger in a wait of unspoken love
And for it to be requited.
I know no such attachment or beauty to come long
I know only what left when it came along

I want to see you before I sleep
As I do before I wake

I will compromise and at times concede
If at times that is what you need
And whether you care not or cannot make time for me
Know that I would like to build a home with tender tenets.
Would you care to be one of my cotenants?
The others haven't made it to this world yet

I shall paraphrase those who say
That this is just a phase
By saying that this is preposterous
For you have put me in a position
Where I must posit
That this posture
Is not just a proposal but a promise
And as I make the remark
That you are the spark
That lit the embers

Of a roaring fire
Cracking wood in the forest
Where they saw force
And called you fierce
But I saw the fairest
Allow me to abbreviate your name to love
And say you would be mine

Pulses of the Stand Alone Complex (Nothing changes)

Seeing how a letter could mean the world
I sent this to you

If you grow a tear to your eye
Nail it to your memory
Keep it with you

Forgive this narrative lead by the interrogative into tergiversation.
Soon the scenario will be a quandary fit for the stalwart
For what spurred this train of thought
Was a broken cog of the engine
That flung me out of the machine with passion

It was not a coincidence that we met twice
We were meant to meet a thousand times more in this life
And into the next; perhaps, even before

How empty are we to believe hollow shells?
Malice lurks in the minds of the weak

At my nadir I tug at a thread with a modicum of force

I propose that something extraordinary happened to us.
I stuck myself onto a perilous journey.
But beware for meeting me leads to treacherous roads.
For your safety, you do not wish to follow me.
You do not wish to cross me.
This is not for the faint of heart
Even less for those who cannot make the leap
But with great hope comes great fear and I fear to break

Some things may unfurl further than I can fathom
As I plead for fate to wait, running around to keep it all together

While run aground all of my plans and my fury turns into a flurry
That starts the whirlwind that spins me endlessly
Like the broken record of a moot moment
With no one to see, no one to hear.
There is nothing more clear
There is nothing, I fear

I find good old salvation for a new found damnation
While still hurt by the vices of the righteous
Witless bullies and hapless punks
Who were curious about the evil that was vicarious

This is only part of a long conversation
That started before our time
And will continue long after it

In the end you only lose one
One battle, one war, one life, one person.
You only lose yourself

If I was to keep quiet or even dare try deceit
Forgive this simple and humble sieve.
Pardon lies in the heart, I hope
For that is where I ask you all to find mine

I go elsewhere without knowing
And I come from there after forgetting
And often I'd catch myself comparing
Two people who were the same person...

Short of fixing humanity
I fancy to clothe randomness
In its most beautiful dress

Read quickly and save yourself some time
Or for just a moment, extend your patience

To find a method to this account of madness

I came to realize what I owe and what I own
I was in awe, I was not alone

Pulses; truth lives and dies
For just us, a simple poetic justice.

A mixture of cohesion and interferences
Fences coming up while others fall flat
Among curves in the courses of energy
The continuation of halted lives through
The duplication without original
The proximity and synchronicity
Of souls that met before
Shape randomness into a pattern

I believe there is no novelty
Just old memories coming back

We never learn a thing.
We simply come to remember
What we knew all along

The constructs I here borrow
Come only to add one more burrow
And quicken the travesty
Of how I try to bury
Things I only wish to be uncovered

I would think of no more serious applications.
Though I may apply myself I can't care to comply
For any more than what I am already committed to

Though there can't be many of those left
I recall moments of introspection

Many a night discussing the very reason why we sat there
Making an inquiry on nature and the nature of men
Amid old voices mixed into one through long loud hums.
In hindsight, this conflation went easily unobstructed.
I am quite acquainted with this trick of the devil.
You see, I believe all demons live to haunt me

I had in mind a different version of life itself.
If all was created, if all was sacred, my dreams remain unholy.
I only wish to be the blade that will cut the firmament
In a crusade where I or it will be slain
Where a people would watch me in awe and disdain
In a long fight believed to be fought in vain
In a steep struggle where there is little to gain.
You can come with me onto this voyage
Of covenants made to build alliances and loyalties
That many would deem unnecessary and mere follies

My composure is not all to blame for what I compose.
I dare not compare the scribbles between times
Where I do or don't shake from emotion
I might though sit beside myself to watch my very motion
The movement sometimes a malady, sometimes a melody
While I carefully compromise my own safety
With a fall flattening beyond belief
That has my verbalized life converted into comic relief
While I weave a broken line of ink
I still laugh at a law that would stoop
To define and constrain my exaltation.
My tongue need not be bolder that my fingers
Since They both linger lying in wait
And suddenly dance to make words out of the silence

I've been here before
The tale of my leave is filled with gore:

A little voice sings while colours dance
A tiny pain stings while I smile in pretense
The chasm moves my very vessel with spams.
I ask that my suffering ends swiftly
If not, that my body heals quickly

What may be the hallmark of the handful that hope?
How long shall I hang here simply because I was given rope?
The abyss at my feet seduces my eyes and steals a tear
But I fail to fall drifting at the horizon of the escaping fear

By each cruelty and each kindness
The eternal recurrence
Plays a tune at a frequency
That transcends our existence.
Between keys ring the notes of music.
This performance always takes in account the public

I dream to wake in each of us what lies
Through this muddy mirror.
Squint your eyes and move through the fog.
Touch the glass and risk to cut yourself.
Touch the crass and risk to dirty yourself

There is no point from which any of us can go back.
We may turn our backs to it all
But there are more turns to the winding path.
Points of reference are illusions

When matter treads
Onto the flow of energy transformations occur.
The strive to alter reality is the quintessence of life.
It's only a matter of convincing one's self

To cross the threshold of conventional boundaries
And reveal ourselves for what cannot be left alone must be met

I may be done here but I am neither done for nor done in.
I step onto the incredible juncture in my adventure
The bifurcation that forces a question onto the great divide.
I will answer it by pressing on in all directions

Life and death are not only carnal, we will meet again.
I not only pray on it, I know it to be my only truth.
May I only open my eyes again in such a world
That would allow it
If even for a short while for I know that would be worthwhile

Farewell, those who fight do not fare well, but that is fair
For no fight is light, not in the light of what kept us in the dark

Despite what another may spout, spare me.
Submitted here is my belief.
Provisions to assess this vision can be found in the heart.
I request that we meet the expectations placed upon us
As undimmed affections in the light of darker things to come
Have us coursing through uncharted territory
Haunted by threats from forces
That never existed and never persisted.
We shall make use of unforgettable words quietly forgotten
In a sea of unnecessary chatter and have them quietly spoken

Errors occurred. Recurrence came from man and history.
Why must we relive the past? To me it's a mystery
I guess nothing changes

But if history is to repeat itself
Let us go back to a time of freedom
A time of revolution

What's harder to teach?
The impossible to believe
Or the impossible to deny?
History will tell

[To be continued, to be repeated]

High Off Contact

Punctuated by the power of the pauses
The plague on the people plays with little trouble
And the roll of rotten fruits brings new roots to causes.
The gain in the losses adds to the pain in the battle

I scat as scatter dots in plots
Of statistics meant for adepts of economics.
I adopt the axioms that transfer through harmonics
In the trade of comics.
It's simple, I am just experimenting with a sample.
I feel numb and then become nimble

I meet with a few cats that hang with acrobats
Rats smoking roaches in flats that fit the cheap chats
That made the bet that a bit of the bite
Is worth the trinkets and treats
Gnawing on bone until they know in their bones
Who eats what meats

Quick movements make the music that slows into noggin.
Around the navel, in turn butterflies churn and level out.
Slaps slip through the cracks with the serpent and the slurping.
Tomorrow they will sweat on mats because the math checks out

Lost in the thoughts of how to set my last supper
A lone drop of liquor helps me find my mind in a stupor
I take the keys to millions worth
Of metal stallions in stupendous stables.
The still is perilous and the road opens to a precipice
So I turn the tables

In the breeze, while I please and tease the squeeze
Unease makes bees buzz in my ears as I step off the trapeze
I close in on a clearing in the clutter

Of syllables stuck in my stutter
And I become a buff of buffers between the birds and the flutter

Lost and Sound

They say I lost it when I found it.
It was safe to say I was still sound.
But by the sound of it I was lost.
I never came to it, it found me.
I was hit at the heart and they thought I was hurt.
They fought my very fight.
They saw a wrong then sought to right it.
But I found peace in the war
A dove in the fire
A dive into desire.
I gave it a shot with my piece
And as I pierce through the fray
I am not afraid to lose myself.
I am not afraid to lose it all.
I cannot imagine I would lose at all.
The curtain calls for the ground
I am lost but I am sound

Wisdom of ancient lovers

Sending drafts to your inbox
Shaking the side of your window
Sounding a chime in your speaker

I've been trying to get in touch with you for months.
I've made the situation seem light
But I doomed myself to dire dares.
I take flight in a dark room and light flares.
For now I touch myself after hours.
A bit of art, some skin and some heart

You're why I watch movies alone
You're why I drive ceaselessly at night
You're why I come in and out of performances
Why I seem to come back from a fight
Why nothing seems right

I have logged in days after days
But you are always away after hours.
I don't know your number and address
And the ancients say I have all the symptoms.
The dashboard has all its lights on, still I drive on

You pulled at my heart
And now each pulse lasts longer
Because you made a run for it with it
And now I feel the stretch of forever.
While I long to slip in the grip of your lips
I read out loud lines for clumsy lovers looking for tips

The grey

I am pensive, painting a picture
With my pencil pointing out my pain out of the strokes
That resemble letters but I draw the shape of pleasure
Because of the wrong measure in my mixture
And black and white fail to mix

I see grey as our misunderstanding of the two superposed
While still opposed in an unfathomable conjecture
Of the plentiful and the void

I find wisdom in the water
In its ties to the moon through tides
Cycles that shape the surface but not the core
That move mountains from shore to shore
The moon that still reflects the coldest light of day.
And I am reminded of a hot kiss from the sun
As I find myself in Icarus
A bit aloof and uncouth if not jealous and callous.
I compose another arrangement
For the music already playing in the universe
And I expand with it faster than I can rehearse.
I still wait for time to run in reverse
But in the meantime, I stretch a smile
Into the truest words I've ever spoken
May they mend me when I am broken.
My eyes catch a glimpse of the glow from a light in the fog.
I grind my teeth at the sound of a breaking hinge of a door
To the ghastly house that hosts ghosts of my time.
I am but a blur of my projection in these space dimensions
I try to ignore what doesn't matter with all of my energy
But I am brought back to it.
Despite my respite, I will respond with an homage and a eulogy.
I see life begin and end in a continuous stream of harmonies.
Reeling in that renewal, I find god on my odd rod

And the system resolves as revolve stars in the night sky
And I close my eyes in the light and simply lie
And for a few minutes I am conscious of being led astray
In the clever convections that add shades and nuances to the grey

A strange sinew

Put your body on my mind why don't you?
I descend to lower levels and start to fiend for you.
I am looking at you like I need to find something in you.
When I get my breath back, I hope I find a friend in you

A strange sinew feeds my need to sin with you.
A sound in the still reveals the strides
Of our bodies moving with the tides
Reminding you I came back each time I withdrew

And we lie, led astray in the fray, holding on something true.
We raise brows and breed anger in the coil of their brew
But I only sip of liquor if it's on your lips you color in blue
And as usual we casually meet in a light with a mystic hue

On the queue to get a clue we got our cue.
And as though we already knew
We had been ready for something new
Prepared by what we, at times, went through

•·•·•·•·•·•·•·•·•·•·•·•·•

.
.
.
.
.
.
.
.
.
.
.

Scribere est loqui at loqui non est scribere.

I thank my family and friends

In particular

Horimbere Jovithe
Thi Minh Tram Nguyen

It was hard for me to pick a title.
I feel like there cannot only be one.
Here are the other names I give to this selection :

- This better be good
- Short of fixing myself
- Loose levies
- The travesty
- Clever clutter
- Nearly nothing
- Far from wisdom
- The words
- The point
- Barely rhyming
- Unbelievable
- The gradients
- Eventually, I write
- Always late
- The damn thing
- Flat paper planes
- Bad origami
- A field for my force
- My mind, so far
- Visions
- You never know
- Highlights of the dark
- Public pleasures
- Odd maneuvers
- One of many names
- Nothing at all